Jazz Play-Along

Book and CD for B♭, E♭, C and Bass Clef Instruments

volume 136

Arranged and Produced by Mark Taylor

NAT ADDERLEY

Cover photo © Riccardo Schwamenthal/CTSIMAGES

ISBN 978-1-4234-9451-5

HAL•LEONARD® CORPORATION
7777 W. BLUEMOUND RD. P.O. BOX 13819 MILWAUKEE, WI 53213

Visit Hal Leonard Online at
www.halleonard.com

NAT ADDERLEY

Volume 136

Arranged and Produced by
Mark Taylor

Featured Players:

Graham Breedlove–Trumpet
John Desalme–Sax
Tony Nalker–Piano
Jim Roberts–Bass
Todd Harrison–Drums

Recorded at Bias Studios, Springfield, Virginia
Bob Dawson, Engineer

HOW TO USE THE CD:

Each song has two tracks:

1) Split Track/Melody

Woodwind, Brass, Keyboard, and **Mallet Players** can use this track as a learning tool for melody style and inflection.

Bass Players can learn and perform with this track – remove the recorded bass track by turning down the volume on the LEFT channel.

Keyboard and **Guitar Players** can learn and perform with this track – remove the recorded piano part by turning down the volume on the RIGHT channel.

2) Full Stereo Track

Soloists or **Groups** can learn and perform with this accompaniment track with the RHYTHM SECTION only.

CD
① : SPLIT TRACK/MELODY
② : FULL STEREO TRACK

HUMMIN'

BY NAT ADDERLEY

C VERSION

THE JIVE SAMBA

BY NAT ADDERLEY

CD
- **7** : SPLIT TRACK/MELODY
- **8** : FULL STEREO TRACK

C VERSION

I SHOULD CARE

WORDS AND MUSIC BY SAMMY CAHN,
PAUL WESTON AND AXEL STORDAHL

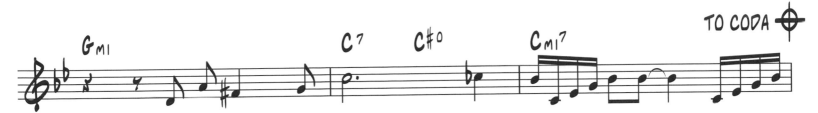

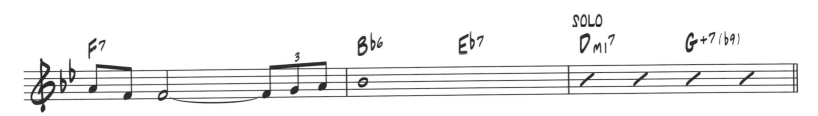

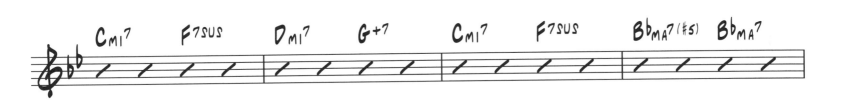

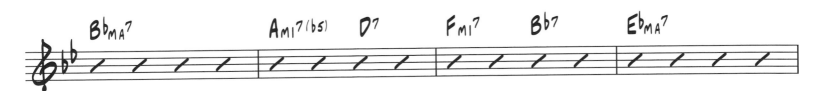

CD

5 : SPLIT TRACK/MELODY	
6 : FULL STEREO TRACK	

C VERSION

I'VE GOT A CRUSH ON YOU

MUSIC AND LYRICS BY GEORGE GERSHWIN
AND IRA GERSHWIN

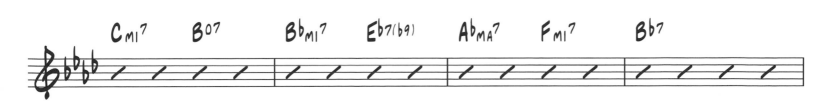

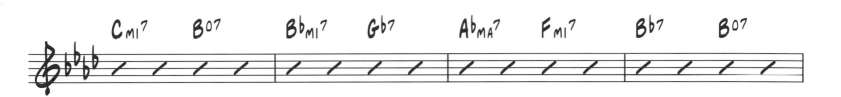

NEVER SAY YES

BY NAT ADDERLEY

CD

⑪ : SPLIT TRACK/MELODY
⑫ : FULL STEREO TRACK

C VERSION

(THE OLD MAN FROM)
THE OLD COUNTRY

BY NAT ADDERLEY
AND CURTIS R. LEWIS

ONE FOR DADDY-O

BY NAT ADDERLEY

CD

13 : SPLIT TRACK/MELODY
14 : FULL STEREO TRACK

C VERSION

CD

⬥15 : SPLIT TRACK/MELODY
⬥16 : FULL STEREO TRACK

C VERSION

TEANECK

BY NAT ADDERLEY

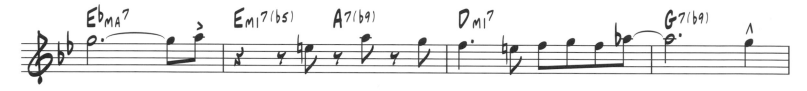

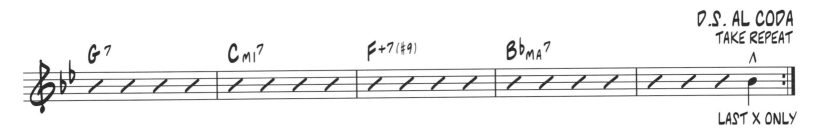

CD
17 : SPLIT TRACK/MELODY
18 : FULL STEREO TRACK

VIOLETS FOR YOUR FURS

BY TOM ADAIR
AND MATT DENNIS

C VERSION

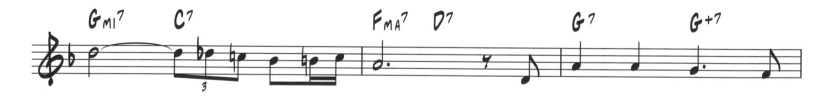

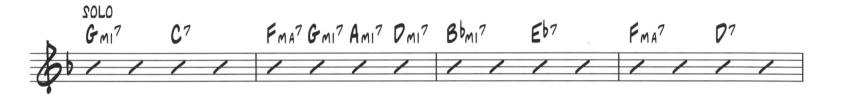

CD

19 : SPLIT TRACK/MELODY
20 : FULL STEREO TRACK

WORK SONG

WORDS BY OSCAR BROWN JR.
MUSIC BY NAT ADDERLEY

C VERSION

HUMMIN'

CD
1 : SPLIT TRACK/MELODY
2 : FULL STEREO TRACK

BY NAT ADDERLEY

Bb VERSION

I SHOULD CARE

WORDS AND MUSIC BY SAMMY CAHN,
PAUL WESTON AND AXEL STORDAHL

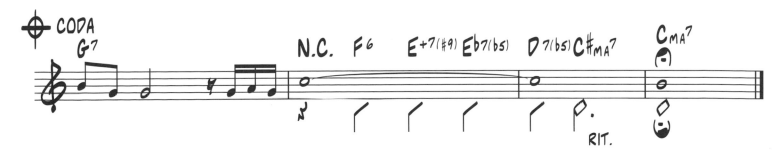

CD

I've Got a Crush on You

MUSIC AND LYRICS BY GEORGE GERSHWIN
AND IRA GERSHWIN

Bb VERSION

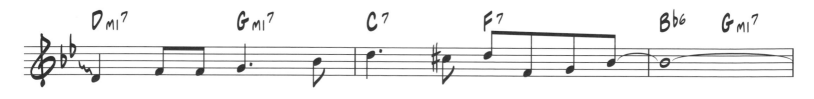

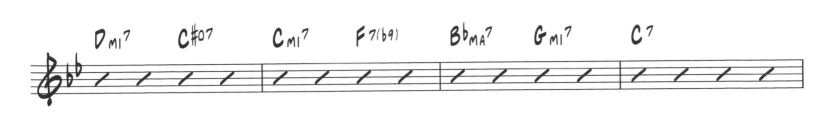

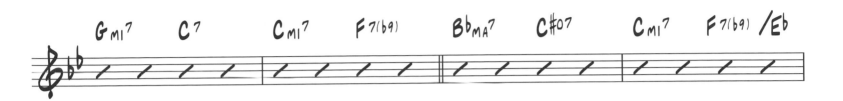

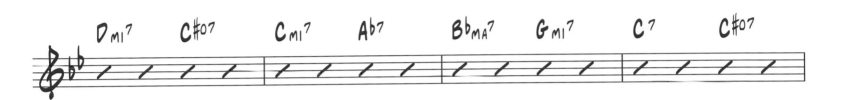

THE JIVE SAMBA

CD
- ◆ 7 : SPLIT TRACK/MELODY
- ◆ 8 : FULL STEREO TRACK

BY NAT ADDERLEY

Bb VERSION

(THE OLD MAN FROM)
THE OLD COUNTRY

BY NAT ADDERLEY
AND CURTIS R. LEWIS

NEVER SAY YES

BY NAT ADDERLEY

Bb VERSION

ONE FOR DADDY-O

BY NAT ADDERLEY

Bb VERSION

WORK SONG

CD
19 : SPLIT TRACK/MELODY
20 : FULL STEREO TRACK

WORDS BY OSCAR BROWN JR.
MUSIC BY NAT ADDERLEY

Bb VERSION

CD

15: SPLIT TRACK/MELODY
16: FULL STEREO TRACK

TEANECK

BY NAT ADDERLEY

Bb VERSION

FAST SWING

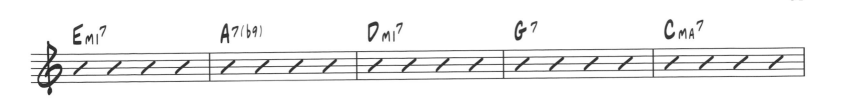

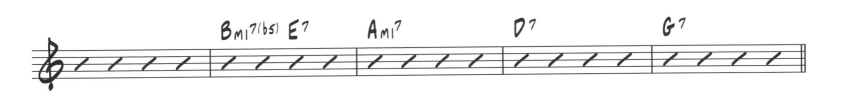

D.S. AL CODA
TAKE REPEAT

LAST X ONLY

CD
17 : SPLIT TRACK/MELODY
18 : FULL STEREO TRACK

VIOLETS FOR YOUR FURS

BY TOM ADAIR
AND MATT DENNIS

Bb VERSION

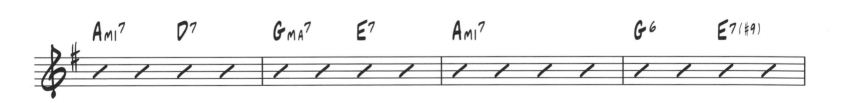

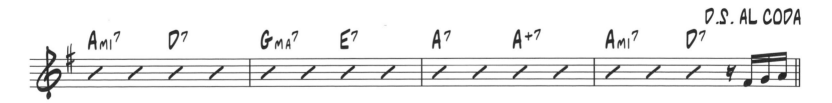

HUMMIN'

CD
1: SPLIT TRACK/MELODY
2: FULL STEREO TRACK

BY NAT ADDERLEY

Eb VERSION

THE JIVE SAMBA

BY NAT ADDERLEY

I SHOULD CARE

WORDS AND MUSIC BY SAMMY CAHN,
PAUL WESTON AND AXEL STORDAHL

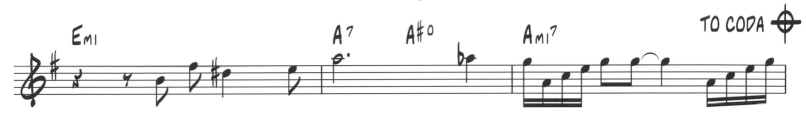

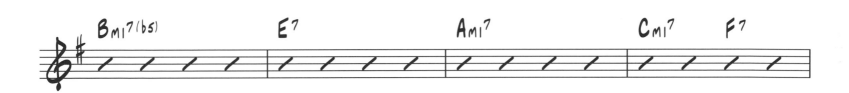

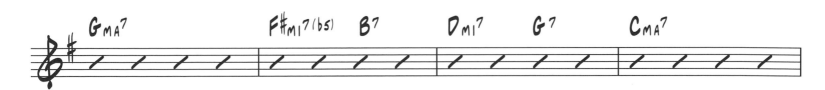

CD
◆ 5 : SPLIT TRACK/MELODY
◆ 6 : FULL STEREO TRACK

Eb VERSION

I'VE GOT A CRUSH ON YOU

MUSIC AND LYRICS BY GEORGE GERSHWIN
AND IRA GERSHWIN

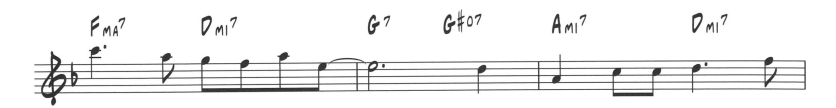

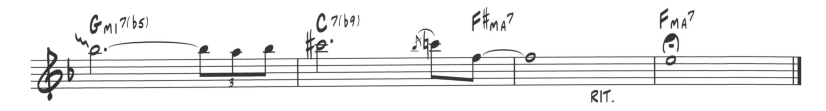

NEVER SAY YES

BY NAT ADDERLEY

Eb VERSION

** CHORDS BOTH X'S

TO CODA

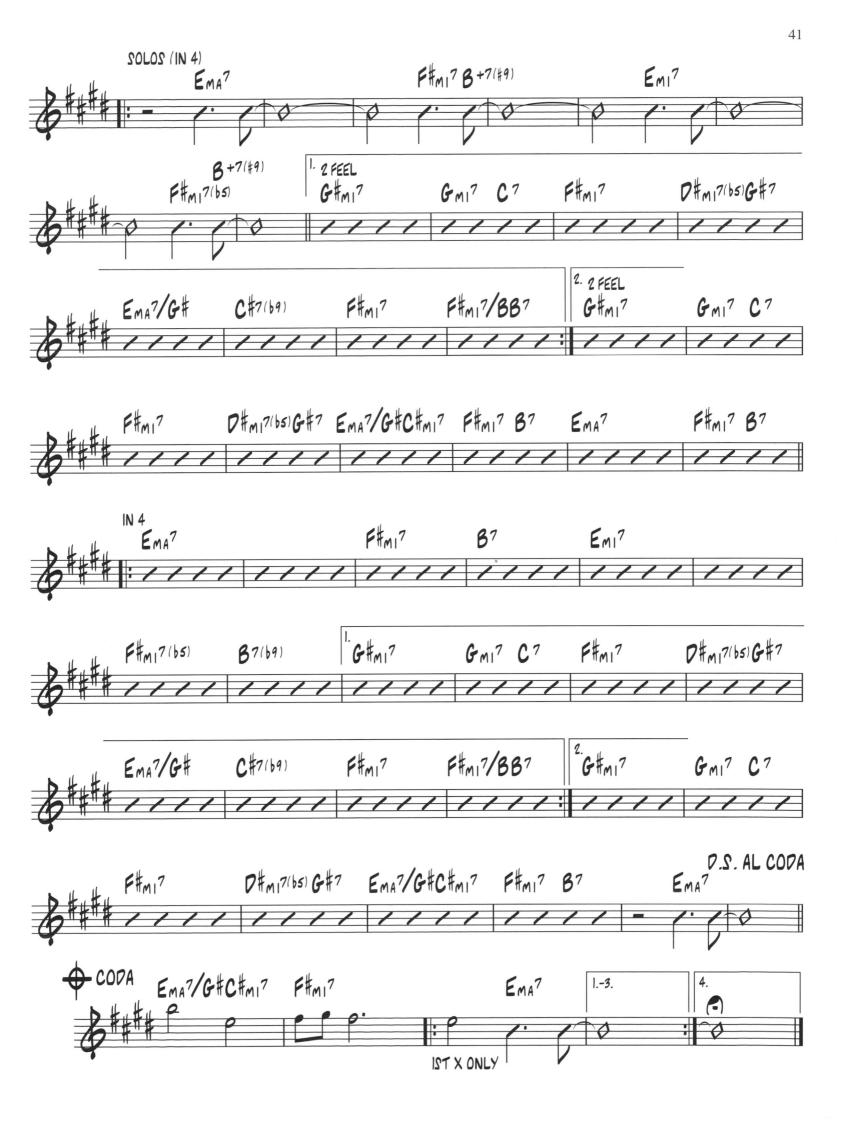

ONE FOR DADDY-O

BY NAT ADDERLEY

Teaneck

BY NAT ADDERLEY

CD
- **15** : SPLIT TRACK/MELODY
- **16** : FULL STEREO TRACK

Eb VERSION

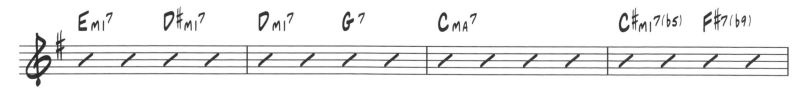

D.S. AL CODA
TAKE REPEAT

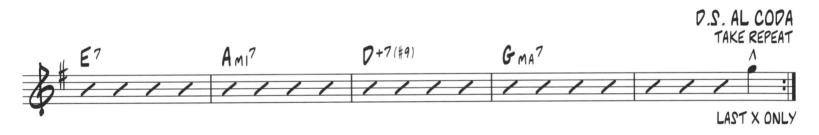

LAST X ONLY

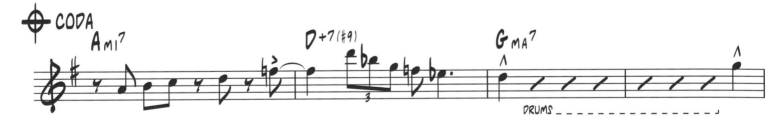

VIOLETS FOR YOUR FURS

CD
17 : SPLIT TRACK/MELODY
18 : FULL STEREO TRACK

BY TOM ADAIR
AND MATT DENNIS

Eb VERSION

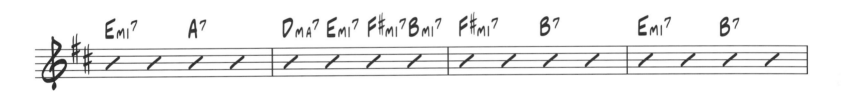

WORK SONG

WORDS BY OSCAR BROWN JR.
MUSIC BY NAT ADDERLEY

CD
19: SPLIT TRACK/MELODY
20: FULL STEREO TRACK

Eb VERSION

MEDIUM SWING

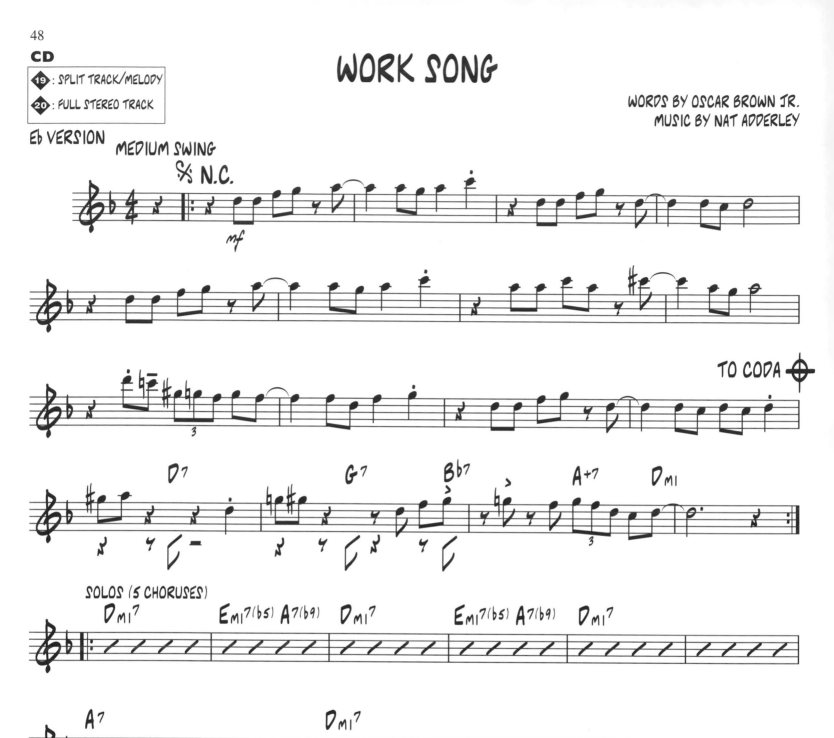

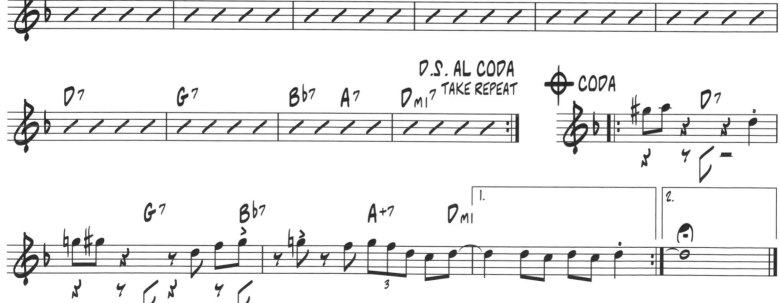

HUMMIN'

BY NAT ADDERLEY

I SHOULD CARE

WORDS AND MUSIC BY SAMMY CAHN, PAUL WESTON AND AXEL STORDAHL

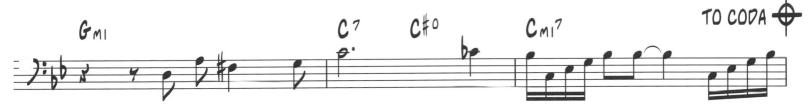

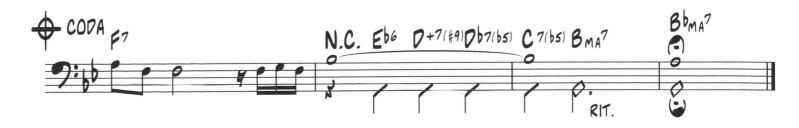

CD
⑤ : SPLIT TRACK/MELODY
⑥ : FULL STEREO TRACK

𝄢: C VERSION

I'VE GOT A CRUSH ON YOU

MUSIC AND LYRICS BY GEORGE GERSHWIN
AND IRA GERSHWIN

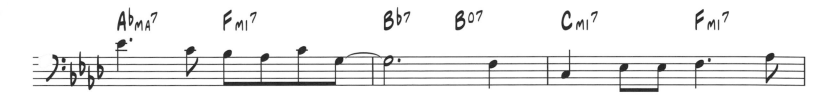

THE JIVE SAMBA

BY NAT ADDERLEY

(THE OLD MAN FROM)
THE OLD COUNTRY

BY NAT ADDERLEY
AND CURTIS R. LEWIS

NEVER SAY YES

BY NAT ADDERLEY

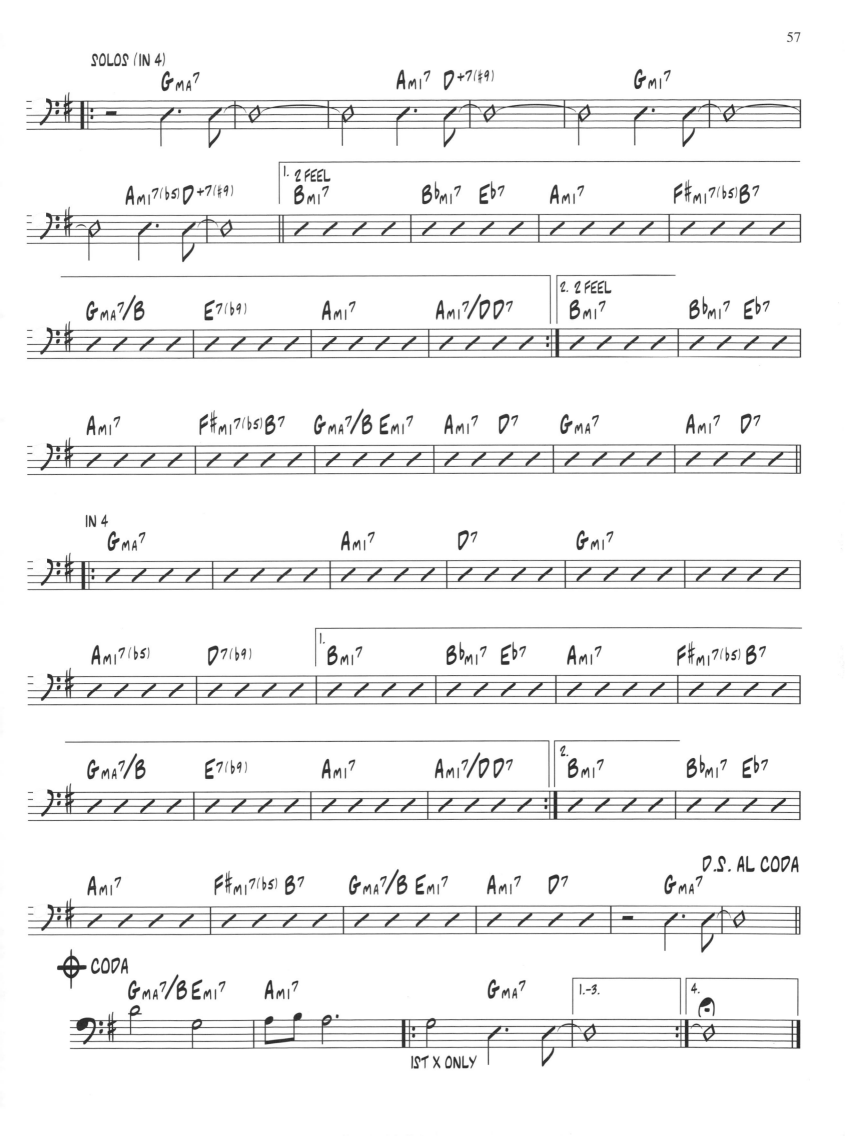

ONE FOR DADDY-O

BY NAT ADDERLEY

WORK SONG

CD
19: SPLIT TRACK/MELODY
20: FULL STEREO TRACK

WORDS BY OSCAR BROWN JR.
MUSIC BY NAT ADDERLEY

C VERSION

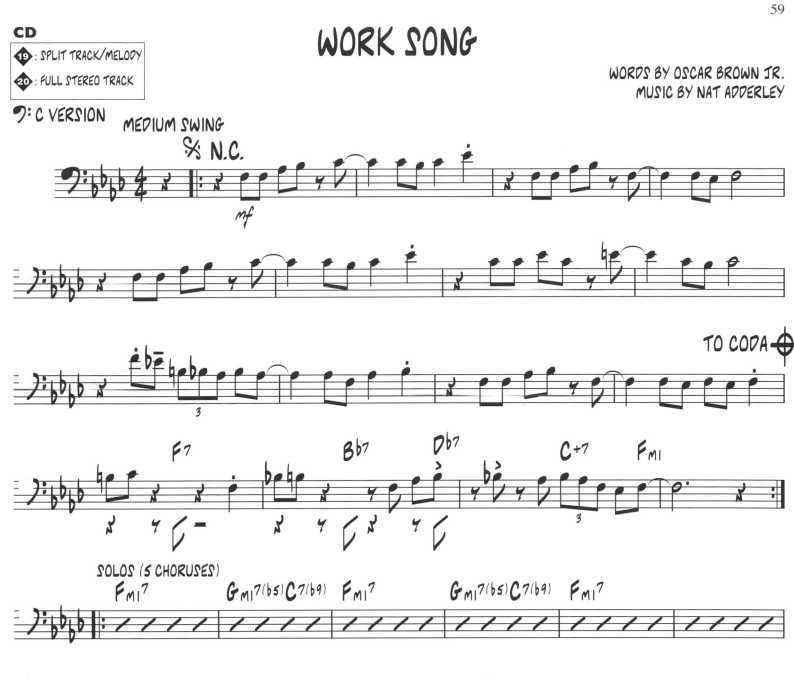

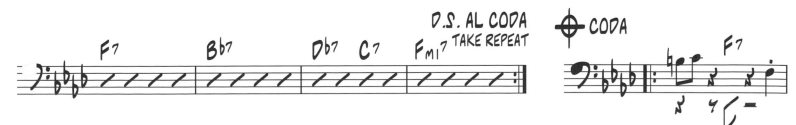

TEANECK

BY NAT ADDERLEY

CD
15 : SPLIT TRACK/MELODY
16 : FULL STEREO TRACK

𝄢 C VERSION

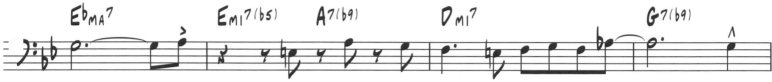

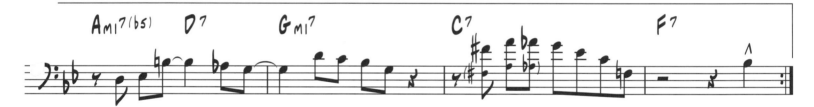

D.S. AL CODA
TAKE REPEAT

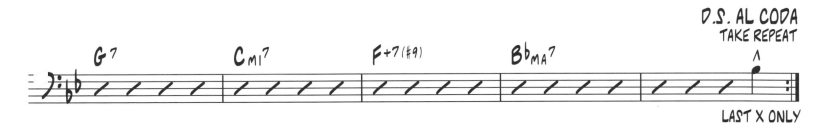

LAST X ONLY

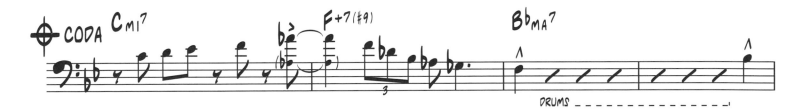

VIOLETS FOR YOUR FURS

BY TOM ADAIR
AND MATT DENNIS

𝄢: C VERSION

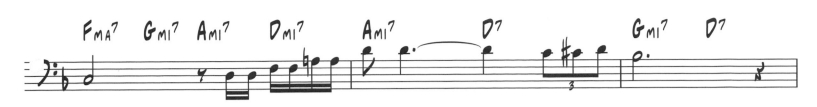

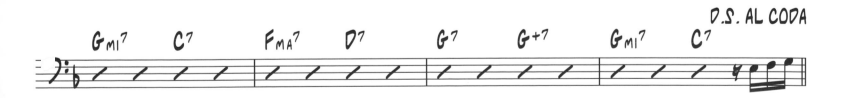

Presenting the Hal Leonard JAZZ PLAY-ALONG SERIES

For use with all B-flat, E-flat, Bass Clef and C instruments, the Jazz Play-Along® Series is the ultimate learning tool for all jazz musicians. With musician-friendly lead sheets, melody cues, and other split-track choices on the included CD, these first-of-a-kind packages help you master improvisation while playing some of the greatest tunes of all time. FOR STUDY, each tune includes a split track with: melody cue with proper style and inflection • professional rhythm tracks • choruses for soloing • removable bass part • removable piano part. FOR PERFORMANCE, each tune also has: an additional full stereo accompaniment track (no melody) • additional choruses for soloing.